Ling Ling

First published in Great Britain 1999 by
Opal Books

Sold and distributed in the UK and Europe by
The Malvern Publishing Company Limited
32, Old Street, Upton upon Severn, Worcestershire, WR8 OHW, England.

North American agent
The British Book Company Incorporated
Web site www://malvernfirst.com
Email bbcpanda@malvernfirst.com

British Library Cataloguing in Publication Data

A catalogue record for this book is available
from the British Library

ISBN 1 902587 04 9

Designed by Dionysia
Produced by The British Book Company Incorporated.

Printed and bound in Malta by Interprint Limited

Ling Ling

THE MOST BEAUTIFUL GIANT PANDA IN THE WORLD

Written by

Bernadette L. Shih

Illustrated by

Dionysia

Dedication

For my son Eric and all children.
To add a little to your joys and help bridge the culture gap.

When I learnt that Washington Zoo had a pair of Giant Pandas, Ling Ling and Hsing Hsing, I was very excited. As a Chinese American born in China, I am always interested in anything that is totally Chinese and what could be more Chinese than the giant panda.

My son was born in America and so I took him to Washington Zoo to see the pandas that were from the land of his ancestors. He was fascinated by them and we watched them for hours. They look like big toys, so cuddly and yet a little sad looking with those big black patches around their eyes.

When we got home Eric could not stop talking about the pandas, and particularly Ling Ling, the young female panda. He kept asking me questions about them and so, at bed time, I made up the story that is in this book.

Eric never tired of hearing the story and whenever I see a panda now I look at it and wonder if perhaps the story is really true.

I hope you will enjoy it as much as Eric did and that you, too, will want to know more about these very rare, very special and very Chinese animals.

Bernadette L Shih, Palos Verdes, California 1999

THE GIANT PANDA

Wild Pandas only live in China

Until recently, none ever left China

Few zoos outside China have Pandas

Very few people have ever seen a live Panda

Pandas do not like having babies in a Zoo

Very few Pandas are left in the world

Pandas only eat bamboo shoots

Pandas are very shy

Pandas do not hurt any other animals

Ling Ling is a girl giant panda who lives in a zoo.
She is two years old and weighs over one hundred and fifty pounds.

Ling Ling has a large den with one wall made of glass.
In the den she has a log pile to sit on and a small house to sleep in.

Every day hundreds of people stand and wait in long lines just to see Ling Ling.
Ling Ling likes to sit near the glass wall and look back at them.

As they pass Ling Ling's den, almost all of them say:
"Isn't she cute!" "Isn't she lovely!" "She is the most beautiful panda!"

They smile and wave. Ling Ling smiles and waves back.
She is so proud of her beauty.

Nothing makes her happier than being thought of as
The Most Beautiful Giant Panda in the World!

One evening, before her friends, Owl, Firefly, Frog, Mouse and Sloth came to visit, Ling Ling smoothed her fur proudly and thought aloud:

"I'm beautiful! I'm The Most Beautiful Giant Panda in the World!
And tonight my friends are coming to help me celebrate my birthday."

Her heart was so filled with happiness, she did a little panda dance.
Around and around and around she twirled.

While Ling Ling was dancing, Owl flew in.
"Happy birthday, Ling Ling!" Owl hooted.

Owl flew all around Ling Ling's den.
Owl always did this to make sure it was safe.

When Owl had checked everywhere,
He settled on the strongest branch of the tree.

Owl, who had very good eyesight, pointed and said:
"What's that over there Ling Ling?"

Ling Ling looked at where Owl was pointing
And saw a faint prick of light.

It was Firefly, gracefully fluttering towards them.
Firefly blinked and flashed a big 'Hello' in the darkness.

Out of nowhere, it seemed, Frog croaked, "Thank you, Firefly!" "If it weren't for your light, I would have hopped right into a skunk!"

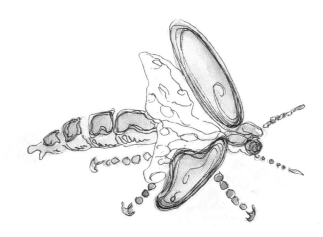

Frog was another friend of Ling Ling's.
"Hello Frog, I am pleased you came." She said.

Ling Ling was getting excited.
Now there were nearly enough friends for her birthday party.

"Speaking of skunk," Mouse squeaked,
"I almost ran into one on my way over!"

All out of breath, Mouse continued. "I'm sorry if I'm late."
"I was trying to wake Sloth up."

"I tried shaking, pushing, and tickling, but it was no use."
"He was still sound asleep, hanging upside down when I left him."

Owl, Firefly, Frog, Mouse and Ling Ling sat quietly, facing each other.
There was nothing they could do but to wait patiently for Sloth to come.

Owl was the first to speak. "Ling Ling, I've always wondered, why, despite your cheerful disposition, you always look so sad! Now I know!"

"It's those black patches you have around your eyes!"
Ling Ling shifted uneasily. "Do I look sad to you too?" She asked the others.

After studying Ling Ling's face carefully,
Firefly, Frog and Mouse nodded their heads.

Then for the first time in her life,
Ling Ling became dissatisfied with her looks.

Before she had a chance to become too unhappy,
Sloth arrived - and her Birthday Party began!

Owl, Firefly, Frog, Mouse and Sloth had brought many presents for Ling Ling.
They helped her blow out the two candles on her birthday cake.

They played games and danced until they were too tired to move.
That night, Ling Ling lay awake on her log pile thinking sad thoughts.

"What can I do about these black patches around my eyes?" She wondered.
And talking to herself, she fell asleep full of unanswered questions.

The next day the zoo keepers did their spring cleaning at the zoo.
A zoo keeper was painting Ling Ling's den.

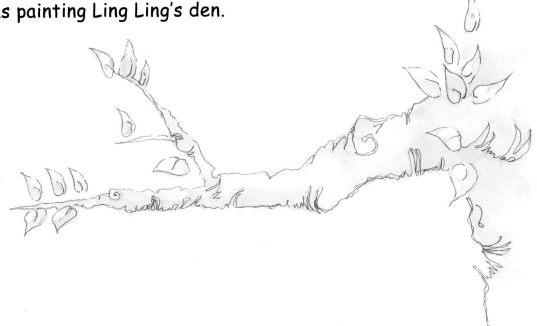

Suddenly, in the middle of a mouthful of bamboo shoots,
the answer Ling Ling was searching for popped into her head.

Ling Ling smeared paint all over her face,
covering the black patches around her eyes with white paint.

Ling Ling was too excited to even eat and spent the whole day playing.
She could hardly wait for her friends, Owl, Firefly, Frog, Mouse and Sloth to come.

Finally, when the moon rose in the sky, Owl arrived.
He turned his head in almost a complete circle as he looked at Ling Ling.

Then he flew away, murmuring to himself.
"Oh dear! Whatever happened to my friend Ling Ling!"

"I must go and warn Firefly and the others.
There is a pale-faced monster in Ling Ling's den!"

Owl was too late. Just as he was flying away, Firefly came.
He took one look at Ling Ling and flew away.

Then Frog, Mouse and Sloth all arrived and saw the white monster.
As soon as they did they all scampered off into the darkness.

Safe and far away from Ling Ling's den,
Frog, Mouse, Owl and Sloth talked about what they had seen.

"There is a fierce polar bear in Ling Ling's place!"
Frog croaked loudly.

"No, it's a giant white-faced monster!" Mouse squeaked.
"A vampire!" Sloth said softly.

Poor Ling Ling was all on her own
and she had to spend the night by herself.

She looked at the full moon above
and felt the cool spring night breeze brush against her cheeks.

Her cheeks felt cold and she wondered why.
It was because tears were streaming down her face.

She fell asleep feeling very sad and lonely.
For the first time her friends were not there to wish her good-night.

For the next two nights, Ling Ling waited for her friends.
But still they did not come.

Ling Ling felt so sad that she cried and cried and cried.
She cried so hard that her tears washed away all the paint on her face.

On the third night, Owl flew by.
He saw the black patches around Ling Ling's eyes, and hooted joyfully.

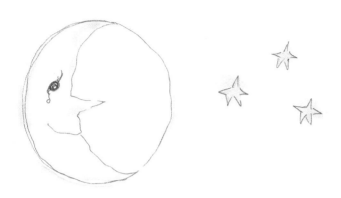

"Ling Ling is back! Ling Ling is back!"
And he flew away to tell the good news to Firefly, Frog, Mouse and Sloth.

Owl quickly came back with Firefly, Frog, Mouse and Sloth.
They were full of tales about the white-faced monster.

Frog croaked. "We were so worried, Ling Ling!"
"We thought the monster was going to live here instead of you."
Ling Ling hung her head in shame, "There was no monster here, it was me all along. I put white paint all over my black patches."

"What did you do a thing like that for!" Owl hooted.
"You are not you Ling Ling, without those black patches around your eyes."
"We like you the way you are, Ling Ling!" Mouse squeaked. And even Sloth, who hardly ever talked, said: "You are beautiful the way you are Ling Ling!"

The six friends, Ling Ling, Owl, Firefly, Frog, Mouse and Sloth all hugged.

Then Firefly blinked long signs in the darkness that said:

LING LING IS THE MOST BEAUTIFUL GIANT PANDA IN THE WORLD!

ling ling is the most beautiful giant panda in the world

From then on, Ling Ling was satisfied with the way she looked.
And she lived happily ever after in the zoo.

Some Facts About The Giant Panda

The Giant Panda is a bear-like animal. It is stockily built and has a very short tail. In fact some scientists think the bear is its closest relative. Its coat is black and white in colour. The dense fur is mainly white with black patches around the eyes and on the shoulders. The legs and ears are also black.

Panda cubs are extremely delicate and small at birth. Like small kittens, they weigh only 3 to 6 ounces when born. When they are fully grown Giant Pandas weigh between 200lbs and 250lbs, more than most men. Even though they are much smaller than the Brown Bear, which they resemble, they are robust creatures with a large heavy body. Although they are heavy and slow in movement, pandas are very playful and love to do somersaults. Since they have extremely flexible bodies, they can twist and turn in many directions. In fact, the Giant Panda is the only mammal that can put its back leg straight up in the air and rest its head on the bottom of its foot.

The panda feeds on the stems and leaves of various species of bamboo. It sometimes hunts for fish and small mammals, but bamboo forms its main diet. Its cheek teeth and an enlarged wristbone are specialized for slicing and crushing food. The Giant Panda may spend as many as 16 hours a day feeding!

The Giant Panda is found in the cold damp bamboo forests of southwestern China which is the only country in the world where it lives in the wild. They live in the bamboo forest zone at an altitude of between 3,500 feet and 10,000 feet. In China the Giant Pandas are called Daxiong Mao, which means Large Bear Cats.

The survival of the Giant Panda is threatened by bamboo die-back over wide areas. Bamboo flowers only about every 40 to 80 years and then dies off. Since this is the panda's chief food, bamboo die-back leads to its starvation. In the late 1980s, pandas suffered high mortality due to this reason. The Giant Panda population is today reduced to only 1,000 in the wild. A rare animal, it is severely threatened by habitat destruction and poaching. Moreover, its way of life confines it to a limited area.

A panda skin can fetch US $100,000 on the black market. Its skin is a prized commodity. Sleeping mats made from a panda skin are believed to allow the sleeper to predict the future and keep ghosts away. Adult pandas are therefore killed for their skins, which are then used to make coats and sleeping mats. The Giant Panda is protected by a variety of Chinese laws whereby poaching or the smuggling of Giant Panda skins is punishable by the death sentence or life imprisonment. However, despite capital punishment being introduced, illegal hunting of this rare animal continues.

The average life span of the Giant Panda is 18 to 20 years in the wild.

The combination of food shortages and illegal hunting cause some people to believe that this beautiful creature may not survive much longer in the wild. Fortunately, scientists and panda lovers all over the world are trying to find ways to increase the number of pandas that are born both in the wild and in zoos.